# Wright Science Pocket Booster

OCR Gateway A
Physics 5, 6, 7 and 8

For GCSE Physics
Higher Tier

For my brother...who taught me resilience through annoying me endlessly as kids and whose photos I stole for some covers!

# How to use this pocket booster

Each topic has a QR code at the end of the page. If you download a free QR code reader on your phone, this will then take you to the video about that topic on YouTube.

If you see a formula in a box – You need to learn it for the exam.

The key idea of this book is to carry it with you and just take those few minutes to read a couple of pages to check you know it. Learn it, revisit it and then review it again. The more you do this, the more information you will retain.

I hope that you find this book useful.

Subscribe to Wright Science on YouTube to for a full set of videos to support you in your GCSE science studies.

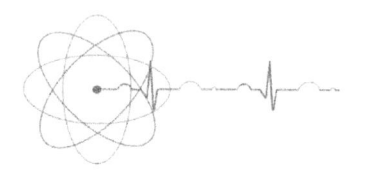

**WRIGHT SCIENCE**
*SCIENCE DONE THE WRIGHT WAY*

ISBN-13: 9781093588071

2019
© Vicki Wright

# P5 Waves in Matter

## P5.1.1: Waves and their Properties

A wave is an oscillation that transfers energy.

There are two types of wave:
1. <u>Mechanical waves</u> (sound and water) need a medium to travel.
2. <u>Electromagnetic waves</u> do not need a medium to travel.

Waves can either be transverse or longitudinal.

In <u>transverse waves</u>, the vibrations are at <u>90°</u> to the direction the wave travels.

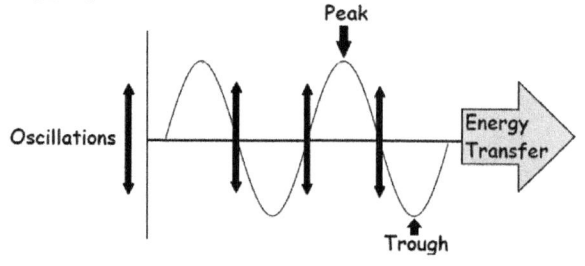

sound waves / ultrasound
noise = longitudinal

In longitudinal waves, the vibrations are in the same direction as the wave travels.

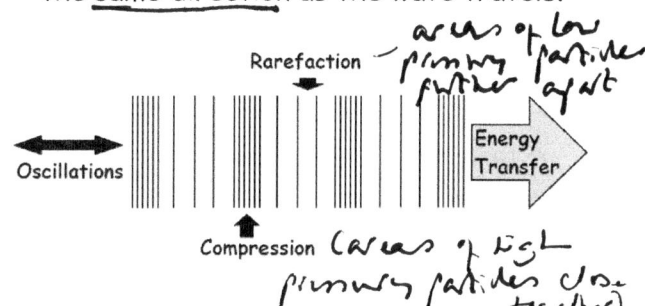

Rarefaction — areas of low pressure, particles further apart

Oscillations ← → 

Energy Transfer →

Compression (areas of high pressure, particles close together)

There are four wave properties we need to know:

1. Amplitude (A) – Distance from the middle to the top or bottom of the wave. Units depend on the wave.
2. Wavelength (λ) – Distance from one point on a wave to the same point on the next wave. Units are metres, m.
3. Frequency (F) – Number of waves or oscillations per second. Units are Hertz, Hz.
4. Time Period (T) – Time for one wave to pass a given point. Units are seconds, s.

7

Waves can be represented as either a time trace or a snapshot. Both graphs allow you to measure amplitude from the middle to the top or bottom of the wave.

A time trace shows how <u>displacement</u> ✗ varies with **time** at a position. We can measure the time period from any point on a wave to the same point on the next.

✱ We can also calculate the time period using
1 ÷ Frequency

A snapshot shows how displacement varies with **distance** at a given time. It allows us to measure wavelength from any point on a wave to the same point on the next.

> *Exam hint: To identify if it is a time trace or snapshot, look at the x axis label.*

## P5.1.2: Wave Velocity

Frequency: Number of waves passing a given point each second.

Wavelength: Distance from one point on a wave to the same point on the next wave.

> **Wave Velocity (m/s) = Frequency (Hz) x Wavelength (m)**

If we wanted to work out the velocity of a sound we can:
- Measure a distance you stand from a wall
- Clap and time how long it takes to hear an echo.
- Use speed = distance ÷ time

Alternatively, we can:
- Connect a pair of microphones a set distance apart to an oscilloscope

- Use the oscilloscope to work out the time between the wave reaching each microphone.
- Calculate the velocity.

The velocity of sound varies with:
- Temperature
- Pressure

## Investigating Waves (PAG P4)

We use a <u>ripple tank</u> to investigate waves. To calculate the velocity of a wave, we need to know the wavelength and frequency.

To measure the wavelength either:
1. <u>Place a ruler</u> in the tank and measure the wavelength.
2. Use a <u>stroboscope</u> to 'freeze' the waves on a piece of paper on the desk below and then use a ruler to measure the wavelength.

To measure the frequency either:
1. Place a marker in the tank and count the waves passing it each second.
2. Place a small piece of paper touching the top of the vibrating bar as it vibrates.   Listen to it and count the vibrations each second.

Do remember that in any technique that involves counting or measuring fast moving objects, humans may make errors.

A safety precaution with the stroboscope – Check for <u>photosensitive people</u> in your group.

## P5.1.3: Sound Properties and Uses

When a wave travels from one medium to another, its velocity can change and so can the direction. This is refraction.

If the wave moves from a <u>less dense medium to a denser medium</u>, the <u>wave slows down and bends towards the normal.</u> The <u>wavelength also decreases but the frequency stays the same.</u>

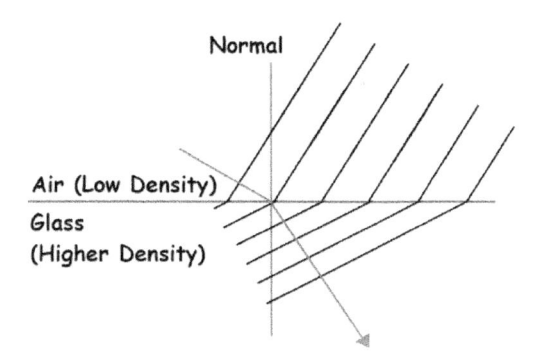

A sound wave that hits the boundary at 0° to the normal will change speed but not direction.

At the boundary, three things can happen. As the wave hits, it is:
1. Reflected (echo)
2. Transmitted (possible refraction)
3. Absorbed

Ultrasound: <u>Sound of a frequency greater than 20,000Hz.</u>
Humans cannot hear ultrasound but other animals can. Ultrasound is useful as it has a short wavelength so it can be focused into a beam.

Ultrasound can be used in medicine <u>to scan unborn babies; monitor blood flow and find kidney stones.</u>

It works by:
- Transmitter beams the ultrasound wave into the patient.
- The <u>waves reflect from the different boundaries</u>.
- The <u>machine calculates the distances</u> using time and velocity and creates an image on the screen.

Echo-sounding and sonar use ultrasound to calculate the depth of water.
E.g. submarines and fishermen

# P5.1.4: Sound in Solids and the Ear

If you shout in an empty room, initially you hear an echo but eventually the sound fades away. The <u>sound is initially reflected</u> to <u>produce the echo</u> and <u>eventually absorbed making the particles in the wall vibra</u>te and makes the wall a bit hotter.

The ear detects, amplifies and converts sound to an electrical signal.

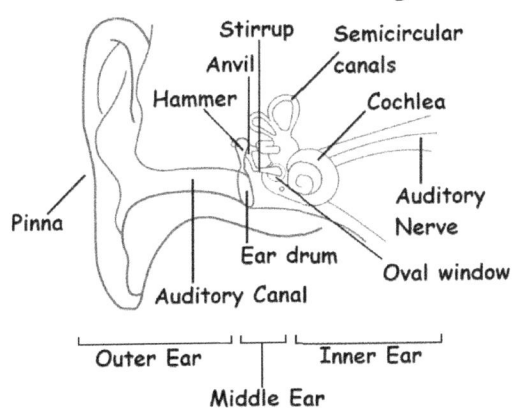

Labels: Stirrup, Anvil, Hammer, Semicircular canals, Cochlea, Auditory Nerve, Oval window, Ear drum, Auditory Canal, Pinna

Outer Ear | Middle Ear | Inner Ear

The pinna and auditory canal (outer ear) gather the sound wave and direct it to the ear drum which vibrates.

As the ear drum vibrates, the ossicles (hammer, anvil and stirrup) vibrate. They also amplify the vibration and pass it to the inner ear through the oval window.

The cochlea is filled with a fluid which transmits the vibrations from the oval window to small hairs on the cochlea wall. The hairs are attached to sound detecting cells that release chemical substances to trigger a nerve impulse down the auditory nerve to your brain.

Your brain processes the signal and you hear the sound.

Natural Frequency: The frequency at which an object oscillates if it is displaced.

Resonance: The large-amplitude oscillation that happens when you make something oscillate at its natural frequency.

The hairs inside the cochlea have different lengths and resonate at different frequencies. The range of hair lengths determines the range of sounds you can hear. The shorter hairs are lost as you get older, so you struggle to hear higher frequencies.

# Check Your Understanding

1. What are the two types of wave?

2. Draw a diagram to show transverse waves.

3. What can be measured on a snap shot?

4. What is the formula for wave velocity?

5. Describe how to use a ripple tank to measure wave velocity.

6. What frequency is ultrasound?

7. Describe how ultrasound is used to produce an image of an unborn baby.

8. Describe how sound travels through the ear.

## P5.2.1: Electromagnetic Waves

When white light passes through a prism, you can see the visible light spectrum. Visible light is part of the electromagnetic spectrum.

The order of waves in the EM spectrum is:

- Radio waves *Raw*
- Microwaves *Meat*
- Infrared (IR) *U*
- Visible light *Very*
- Ultraviolet (UV) *Unusual*
- X-Rays *X-type*
- Gamma Rays *Giraffe*

This shows the waves in increasing frequency and decreasing wavelength.

<u>Electromagnetic waves consist of oscillating electric and magnetic fields.</u> The fields oscillate at 90° to the direction of the wave.

EM waves = Transverse.
E.T.

All EM waves travel through a vacuum at $3.0 \times 10^8$ m/s. This is also the speed of light as it is part of the EM spectrum.

Sources emit EM waves e.g. microwave ovens emit microwaves. Objects also absorb EM waves e.g. skin absorbs infrared to heat up. EM waves transfer energy from sources to absorbers.

Radio waves are produced when an oscillating potential difference across a wire makes electrons move backwards and forwards. This produces a changing electric and magnetic field which is emitted as a radio wave.

Radio waves are detected as when the fields meet a piece of metal, the electrons move and an electrical signal is produced.

## P5.2.2: EM Radiation Uses and Dangers

EM radiation is used in the following:
- Microwaves are used in mobile phones; satellites; Wi-Fi and Bluetooth.
- Radio waves are used in radio and TV.
- Infrared is used in remote controls and optical fibres.
- Visible light can be used to communicate between ships.
- Lasers in CDs, DVDs and Blu-rays use visible light to read the discs.
- X-rays can kill cancer cells and also produce images of bones.
- Gamma rays can kill bacteria and cancer cells.

Ultraviolet is useful for:
- The body producing vitamin D which you need for strong bones.
- Forensics officers identifying forged bank notes and find bodily fluids.
- Sterilising water by killing bacteria.

EM waves can also be used to transfer energy to cook food in two ways:

1. Microwave ovens emit microwaves which are absorbed by the fat and water in the food. They can penetrate a few centimetres into the food. The energy is then transferred by conduction to the middle.

2. Infrared radiation is absorbed by the particles on the surface of the food. The energy is then transferred by conduction to cook the rest of the food. Therefore, conventional ovens are slower at cooking food than microwaves.

## Dangers

Ultraviolet can <u>damage the DNA in skin cells leading to skin cancer</u>. Too much exposure to UV light in your eyes can lead to cataracts.

<u>X-rays can damage cells</u> and cause cancer. Radiographers stand behind a lead screen or leave the room to reduce exposure. They also <u>wear a badge</u> that changes when the safe exposure limit has been reached.

Gamma rays can also kill or damage cells in the body.

# P5.2.3: Imaging with EM Waves

## Infrared

Thermal imaging cameras produce a thermogram. Pixels inside a charge-coupled device (CCD) absorb infrared radiation and produce an image. The colours are then added by a computer. Hotter areas emit more infrared radiation.

## X-Rays

Bones absorb X-rays but soft tissue does not. When photographic film absorbs X-rays, it darkens. This allows us to identify broken bones.

A CCD can also detect X-rays. The colours show the different densities of material. The higher the density, the more X-rays are absorbed. Computerised Tomography (CT) scans are used to look inside the body.

## Gamma Rays

Gamma rays are used a tracers in medicine. A tracer is injected, swallowed or inhaled and a scanner then detects the gamma rays emitted. A computer provides an image.

Gamma rays can also be used a tracers in underground pipes. A greater concentration of gamma rays are found at the source of the leak.

## Check Your Understanding

1. List the waves of the electromagnetic spectrum, starting with the longest wavelength.

2. What speed does ultraviolet travel at?

3. Explain how radio waves are produced.

4. Explain why microwaves cook food faster than infrared.

5. List two uses and two dangers of electromagnetic waves.

6. Describe two imaging techniques that use electromagnetic waves.

# P5.3.1: EM Waves and Matter

Ray diagrams are used to show reflection and refraction.

Key Points:
1. Use a RULER!
2. Draw lines to represent the rays.
3. Draw the normal at 90° to the surface at the point the ray hits it.
4. Measure the angles between the normal and the rays.
5. Add arrows to show the direction.

When light enters a denser medium at an angle, it slows down and bends towards the normal. The greater the difference in density, the greater the change in direction. This is refraction. We can use what we observe with light to explain the other EM waves as they behave in the same way.

If we want to transmit waves across large distance on Earth, there is a problem as the Earth is curved. To send radio waves a long distance, they are reflected from the ionosphere (part of the atmosphere).

High-frequency radio waves or microwaves are used for satellite communications as they pass through the ionosphere.

The wavelength determines what happens to EM waves:

- Walls transmit radio waves and microwaves but absorb visible light and ultraviolet.
- The atmosphere absorbs X-rays and gamma rays which protects us from them.

# P5.3.2: Lenses

We have two types of lenses:

1. Convex (converging) lenses refract rays to a principal focus or focal point. They are used in magnifiers.

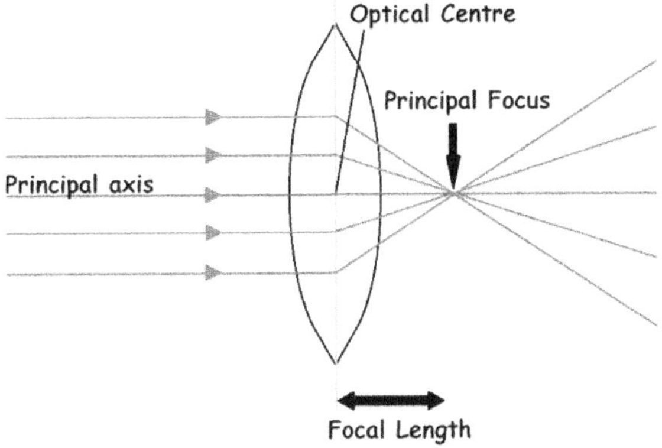


Focal length is the distance from the optical centre to the principal focus.

2. Concave (diverging) lenses spread light out.

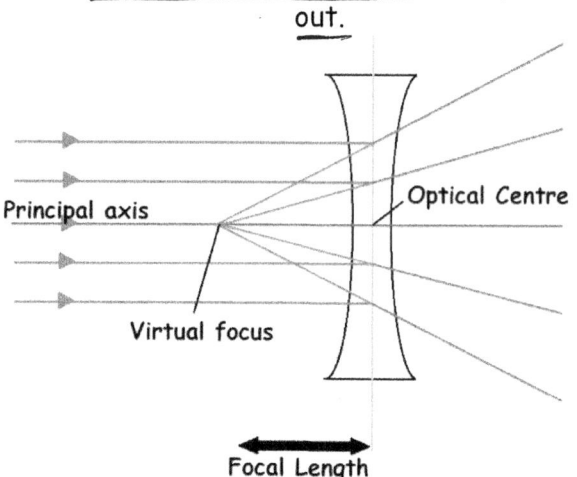

*Principal axis — Optical Centre — Virtual focus — Focal Length*

Focal length is the distance from the virtual focus to the optical centre.

We commonly use lenses in glasses to correct vision problems.

Short sight (distant objects blurry) – Rays focus in front of the retina. Concave lens spreads the rays out so they focus on the retina.

Long sight (near objects blurry) – Rays focus behind the retina. Convex lens refracts the rays in so they focus on the retina.

Drawing ray diagrams with lenses:
1. Draw a ray from the top of the object to the lens parallel to the principal axis.
2. Draw a ray from the lens through the principal focus.
3. Draw a ray from the top of the object through the centre of the lens.

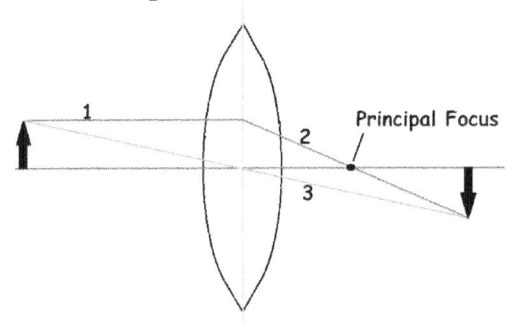

Convex lenses are used for:
- Magnifying glass – Creates a virtual, magnified and upright image
- Camera – Creates a real, diminished and inverted image
- Projector – Creates a real, diminished and inverted image

Concave lenses are used for spy holes and coach rear windows. They both create a virtual, diminished and upright image.

## P5.3.3: Light and Colour

If you shine white light through a prism, it is split into the spectrum. This is because each frequency of light travels at a different speed in glass and is refracted by a different amount. The higher the frequency, the greater the degree of refraction. This effect is called dispersion. The colours associated with the different frequencies in white light are known as the spectral colours.

The retina inside your eye is sensitive to red, green and blue frequencies of light. The receptor cells detect the frequencies and the brain interprets the signals sent to make perceived colour.

We can use filters to change the light that is visible. A filter will absorb all frequencies of white light except for those that match the colour of the filter.

E.g. A red filter will absorb all frequencies but the red. Red light is transmitted.

If we place two different colour filters in front of our light source, then all frequencies are absorbed so objects look black.

If we have a green ball in white light, the ball looks green as it absorbs all frequencies of light except green which is reflected.

If we look at the same ball under red light, it will appear black as the red frequency is absorbed and there is no green frequency to be reflected.

Reflection is dependent on the type of surface. A mirror allows you to see sharp images as the reflection is specular (regular). You cannot see images in paper as paper has diffuse scattering of light.

Light can be scattered from particles. For example, milk appears white as the particles scatter all wavelengths, but ink appears black as the particles absorb all wavelengths.

The molecules in the atmosphere are very small so only scatter light with short wavelengths (blue) so the sky looks blue.

# Check Your Understanding

1. Describe how to draw a ray diagram.

2. Explain why light is refracted as it passes from air into glass.

3. What type of EM radiation do we use to transmit to satellites in orbit?

4. Draw a ray diagram for a convex lens.

5. Draw a ray diagram for a concave lens.

6. Explain how a lens could be used to correct long sight.

7. Describe the image produced in a camera.

8. What colour would a red book appear under green light? Explain your answer.

# P6 Radioactivity

## P6.1.1: Atoms and Isotopes

The nucleus of an atom is made up of protons and neutrons. The charge on the nucleus depends on the number of protons present. It is always positive.

| Subatomic Particle | Relative Mass | Relative Charge |
|---|---|---|
| Proton | 1 | +1 |
| Neutron | 1 | 0 |
| Electron | 0.0005 | -1 |

<u>Isotope: Atom with the same atomic number but a different mass number</u> because it has the same number of protons and electrons but a different number of neutrons. E.g. Carbon-12, Carbon-13 and Carbon-14

$$^{12}_{6}C \quad ^{13}_{6}C \quad ^{14}_{6}C$$

Each has 6 protons.
C-12 has 6 neutrons; C-13 has 7 neutrons and C-14 has 8 neutrons.

Atomic Number: Number of protons OR the number of electrons.

Mass Number: Number of protons + Number of neutrons

If asked to work out the number of protons or electrons in an atom, write down the atomic number from the periodic table.

If asked to work out the number of neutrons of an atom, subtract the atomic number from the mass number.

## P6.1.2: Alpha, Beta and Gamma

Most atoms are stable – They do not decay. <u>Atoms with an unstable nucleus will emit radiation as they decay.</u> A material that emits radiation is radioactive.

There are four types of radiation:
1. Alpha particles (α) – Nucleus of a helium atom, $^4_2He$.
2. Beta particles (β) – Fast moving electrons, $^0_{-1}e$.
3. Gamma waves (γ) – Wave of the electromagnetic spectrum.
4. Neutron particles (n) – Particle in the nucleus, $^1_0n$. – ru. – man. – charge.

For the symbols, the top number is the mass relative to a proton and the bottom number is the charge.

The nucleus doesn't contain electrons, so the beta particle is formed from the decay of a neutron forming a proton and an electron.

If we need to detect radiation, <u>we use a Geiger-Müller tube or Geiger counter</u>. The <u>clicks</u> that are heard are <u>tiny currents produced when the radiation ionises atoms of the gas inside the tube</u>.

Radiation emitted by radioactive material is ionising radiation. Ionising radiation can remove electrons from atoms to produce positively charged ions. To ionise an atom, energy must be transferred to it. Alpha particles transfer more energy to the material they travel through hence, their short range.

# Alpha, beta and gamma have different penetrating powers.

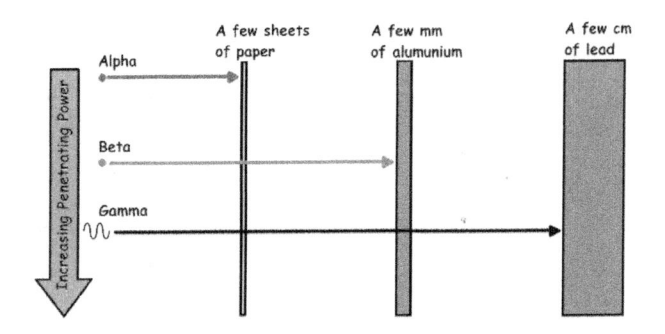

Increasing Penetrating Power

Alpha — stopped by a few sheets of paper

Beta — stopped by a few mm of alumunium

Gamma — stopped by a few cm of lead

## Key Properties of Radiations

Alpha
Relative mass: Large
Charge: +2
Ionising Power: High
Range: Short

Beta
Relative mass: Small
Charge: -1
Ionising Power: Medium
Range: Medium

Gamma
Relative mass: None
Charge: None
Ionising Power: Low
Range: Long

## P6.1.3: Nuclear Equations

### Alpha Decay
An alpha particle is emitted which is made of two protons and two neutrons (helium nucleus).

$$^{240}_{94}Pu \rightarrow {}^{236}_{92}U + {}^{4}_{2}He$$

The mass decreases by 4 and the atomic number decreases by 2 so a new element is formed.

### Beta Decay
A neutron decays to a proton and an electron.

$$^{14}_{6}C \rightarrow {}^{14}_{7}N + {}^{0}_{-1}e$$

The mass does not change as the total number of protons and neutrons remains the same (1 neutron is lost but 1 proton is gained). The atomic number increases by 1 so a new element is formed.

## Gamma Decay

Gamma rays are electromagnetic waves and have no mass or charge. This means there is no change in the mass number or atomic number.

## Neutron Emission

The decay of some nuclei leads to the production of large numbers of neutrons. These neutrons are then emitted to make it stable.

E.g. helium-5

$$^5_2He \rightarrow {}^4_2He + {}^1_0n$$

*Exam hint: If you know the symbols for the types of radiation, you can work out whatever else is missing from the question.*

## P6.1.4: Half-Life

Radiation is emitted at random. A Geiger counter can be used to measure the radiation. This measures the activity. Activity (Count): Radiation emitted per second. Measured in Becquerels (Bq).

Half-Life: Time it takes for the activity to halve. It is also the time it takes for half the unstable nuclei to decay. The half-life of a material may be long or short.

There are two ways to calculate half-life.
1. Using calculations:
E.g. A sample of radon-222 has an activity of 100Bq. Calculate the activity after 11.4 days. The half-life of radon-222 is 3.8 days.
Step 1: Calculate the number of half-lives.
11.4 ÷ 3.8 = 3 half-lives
Step 2: Calculate the new activity.
($\frac{1}{2} \times \frac{1}{2} \times \frac{1}{2}$) × 100 = 12.5Bq

2. From a graph:
- Look at the total activity on time 0.
- Divide it by 2.
- Draw a horizontal line across from this number to the curve.
- Where the line meets the curve, draw a vertical line to the time axis and read off the value.

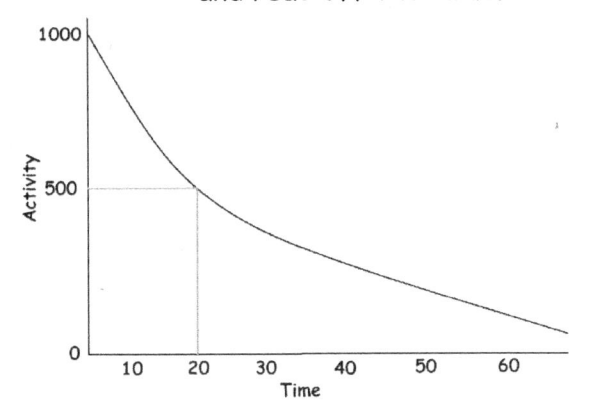

## P6.1.5: Radiation in and out of Atoms

Electrons occupy certain energy levels around the nucleus. Different atoms have different energy levels. Electrons usually occupy the lowest possible energy level (the smallest distance from the nucleus).

In the photon model, electromagnetic radiation is emitted and absorbed as packets of energy called photons. The energy of each photon is proportional to the frequency. In order to excite an electron to a higher energy level, a photon of the right energy must be absorbed. Once the photon has been absorbed, the electron moves to the higher energy level and the atom is in an excited state.

If light of all frequencies is passed through hydrogen gas, some frequencies are absorbed and an absorption spectrum is produced which shows a set of frequencies of radiation absorbed by an atom when excited electrons move to higher energy levels. The black lines are the frequencies absorbed.

A photon that has enough energy can completely remove an electron from the atom. This atom is ionised. Photons of UV, X-ray and gamma ray frequencies have enough energy to ionise atoms.

When electrons move from a higher to lower energy level, they emit radiation. An emission spectrum shows a set of frequencies of radiation emitted by an atom when excited electrons move to a lower energy level. The frequency of radiation emitted depends on the difference in energy of the energy levels.

This energy change can take place in one go or two or more. If it occurs over two or more, then the emitted photons will have less energy, lower frequencies and longer wavelengths.

The largest energy difference is from an energy level just below ionisation. This will vary in different atoms:
E.g.
Hydrogen can emit UV photons
But
Carbon can emit X-ray photons.

Protons and neutrons occupy energy levels in the nucleus and can emit gamma rays as the energy involved is much higher.

## Check Your Understanding

1. What is the relative mass and relative charge on each subatomic particle?

2. Define the term isotope.

3. Describe the four types of radiation.

4. Compare the penetrating and ionising powers of alpha, beta and gamma radiation.

5. Describe the four types of decay, including the equations.

6. Define the term half-life.

7. Explain how to calculate half-life.

8. Describe how an absorption spectrum is formed.

## P6.2.1: Radiation and the Human Body

Background radiation is made up of sources of radiation that we are exposed to all the time. Background radiation comes from:
- Radon gas 50.0%
- Medical uses 14.0%
- Ground and buildings 14.0%
- Food and drink 11.5%
- Cosmic rays 10.0%
- Other 0.2%
- Nuclear weapon tests 0.2%
- Nuclear power 0.1%

Contamination – Occurs when radioactive material is taken inside the body or on the skin. Internal contamination cannot be removed.

Irradiation – Occurs when radioactive material is outside your body. The radiation can travel into the body.

The problem of radiation is that when it enters the body, the DNA inside the cells can be damaged and this can lead to cancer. Radioactive materials are a hazard but the risk of cancer as a result of exposure to low doses is very low. Small doses of radiation lead to damage that can be repaired by the body.

Medical Tracers:
- Radioactive isotope is injected, inhaled or swallowed.
- Gamma camera is used to detect the radiation to show problems in the body.

Radiographers must choose the isotope carefully to ensure the half-life is not too short or too long and that it emits the right type of radiation.
E.g. Technicium-99 is absorbed by a range of organs and has a half-life of around 6 hours.

# Gamma Knife:

## The gamma knife is used to treat some cancers.

It is a moveable source of gamma radiation is moved around the body but focused on the tumour. This reduces the dose healthy cells receive preventing their death but gives a high enough dose to the tumour to kill those cells.

## P6.2.2: Nuclear Fission

Unstable nuclei emit radiation. The nucleus can emit alpha particles, beta particles, gamma rays or neutrons.

Nuclear fission is where a large nucleus is split into smaller nuclei and neutrons. It does not often occur spontaneously. If the nucleus absorbs a neutron, fission is more likely.

The nucleus splits to produce 2 smaller nuclei and 2 or 3 neutrons.
E.g. Uranium-235 and Uranium-239 are fissionable (split easily).

Nuclear power stations use fission to heat water to produce the steam to drive the turbines and generators. The energy transferred to the surroundings via fission is much greater than the energy transferred in a combustion reaction.

Each nucleus that splits, releases 2 or 3 neutrons. These neutrons can then trigger other fission reactions. This is a chain reaction if it is left uncontrolled.

A chain reaction can only occur if there are enough nuclei around the first nuclei. A small mass of radioactive material would result in the neutrons escaping and the reaction stopping.

Chain reactions are controlled in nuclear power stations by the use of control rods. These rods absorb the neutrons.

In a nuclear bomb, there is not control of fission leading to a huge amount of energy being transferred quickly.

> *Exam hint: Remember in fiSSion nuclei SplitS*

## P6.2.3: Nuclear Fusion

Nuclear fusion is where two lighter nuclei join to make a more stable nucleus.

In our Sun, hydrogen nuclei (protons) fuse together to form larger nuclei. Hydrogen nuclei fuse to make helium. These can then fuse and eventually make carbon, oxygen and iron. During these reactions, energy is transferred from the nuclear store by heating and EM radiation.

The problem with nuclear fusion is the repulsion caused by both protons being positive must be overcome.

Fusing protons:
Two protons fuse to form deuterium or hydrogen-2.
Deuterium can be fused to make tritium or hydrogen-3.

Hydrogen-2 and hydrogen-3 fuse to form helium and a neutron. Helium is more stable than the isotopes of hydrogen it is made from.

Iron is the heaviest element made by fusion. Elements heavier than iron are made in a supernova.

Fusion can occur in the Sun due to:
- High temperatures – Increase the speed at which the nuclei are moving
- High pressures – keep the nuclei close enough to fuse together.

It is hard to achieve these conditions on Earth so nuclear fusion reactors as a source of energy as still non-existent.

> Exam hint: Remember in f**U**sion nuclei **U**nite

The mass of the products of fusion, helium and a neutron, is slightly less than the mass of the reactants, hydrogen-2 and hydrogen-3. This very small mass produces a lot of energy in the form of radiation. You can calculate the amount of energy using the formula:

$$E = \Delta m c^2$$

E = Energy (J)
$\Delta m$ = change in mass (kg)
c = speed of light (300 million m/s)

As the speed of light is so large, converting tiny masses to energy generates huge amounts of energy.

## Check Your Understanding

1. List three sources of background radiation.

2. Explain the difference between contamination and irradiation.

3. Explain how the half-life of a tracer is selected.

4. Explain the process of nuclear fission.

5. Explain the difference between a nuclear bomb and a nuclear reactor.

6. Explain the process of nuclear fusion.

# P7 Energy

## P7.1.1: Energy Stores and Energy Transfers

Energy is a quantity in joules (J) that tells you what is possible but does not tell you what will happen.

There are 8 energy stores you need to remember and their related formulae:

1. <u>Chemic</u>al store e.g. glucose in your muscles or a fuel with oxygen.

2. <u>Thermal</u> store e.g. a hot bath
Energy (J) =
Mass (kg) × SHC (J/kg°C) × Temperature Change (°C)

3. <u>Kinetic</u> store e.g. moving car

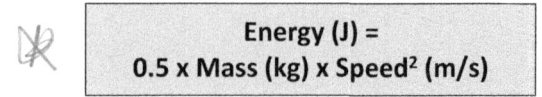

> **Energy (J) =**
> **0.5 × Mass (kg) × Speed² (m/s)**

4. Gravitational store e.g. diver standing on a diving board

> Energy (J) =
> Mass (kg) x g (N/kg) x Height (m)

5. Elastic store e.g. stretched elastic band

Energy (J) = 0.5 x Spring Constant (N/m) x Extension² (m)

6. Nuclear store e.g. Uranium-235

Energy (J) = Change in Mass (kg) x Speed of light² (m/s)

7. Electrostatic store e.g. two opposite charges held apart

8. Magnetic store e.g. two opposite poles of a magnet held apart

There are <u>four ways that energy</u> is <u>transferred between the stores</u>:
1. Mechanically
2. Electrically
3. Heating by particles
4. Heating by radiation

We can calculate the energy transferred mechanically using the formula:

**Work Done (J) = Force (N) x Distance (m)**

We can calculate the energy transferred electrically using the formula:

**Energy Transfer (J) = Power (W) x Time (s)**

Energy cannot be created or destroyed. It can only be transferred between stores. This is the law of conservation of energy. Closed systems will have no net energy change.

## P7.1.2: Energy Analysis with Forces 1

To carry out an energy analysis you need to:
- Choose 2 points in a process
- Identify which stores have more or less energy in them at those points.
- Work out which type of transfer has occurred between the stores.

Example: A racing car
At the start of the race:
Stationary car – Kinetic store is empty
There is lots of fuel and oxygen – Chemical store has lots of energy

At the end of the race:
Moving car – Kinetic store has some energy
There is less fuel and oxygen – Chemical store has less energy

Transfer:
Engine exerting a force – Mechanically

We can represent this on an energy analysis diagram.

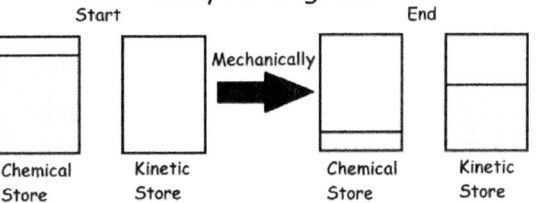

*Start — Chemical Store, Kinetic Store → Mechanically → End — Chemical Store, Kinetic Store*

In a closed system, the decrease in energy in the chemical store is equal to the increase in the kinetic store due to the mechanical work done.

In reality, not all energy is transferred to kinetic energy. Some energy is transferred to the thermal store due to friction, sound or air resistance.

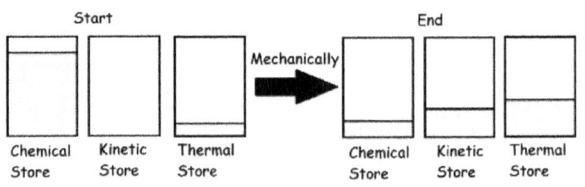

*Start — Chemical Store, Kinetic Store, Thermal Store → Mechanically → End — Chemical Store, Kinetic Store, Thermal Store*

You may be asked to use the formulae you have learnt over the physics course to calculate energy changes.

E.g. A drag racer, starting from rest, exerts a force of 4000N over 300m. Calculate the work done. The mass of the racer is 300kg, calculate the final speed.

Step 1: Identify the formula to use
Work Done = Force x Distance

Step 2: Substitute in and solve
Work Done = 4000 x 300 =1,200,000J

Step 3: Identify the next formula to use.
Kinetic Energy = 0.5 x Mass x Speed$^2$

Step 4: Rearrange, substitute in and solve.
Speed = $\sqrt{(2E \div m)}$
= $\sqrt{(2 \times 1,200,000 \div 300)}$ = 90m/s

## P7.1.3: Energy Analysis with Forces 2

Brakes exert a force on a car which results in energy being transferred from the kinetic store to the thermal store.

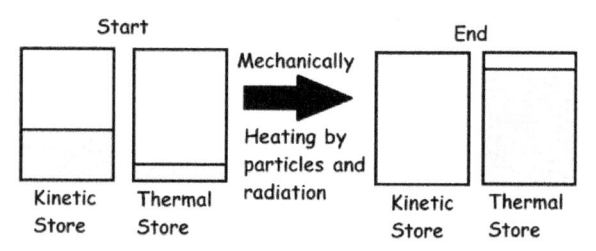

Start → Mechanically, Heating by particles and radiation → End

Kinetic Store, Thermal Store → Kinetic Store, Thermal Store

Here the car is moving initially and the surroundings are cool so there is some energy in the kinetic store and thermal store. After the brakes have been applied, the car stops and the brakes heat up due to friction.

A gymnast jumping on a springboard would have an energy analysis as follows:

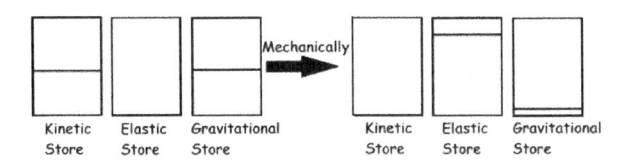

| Kinetic Store | Elastic Store | Gravitational Store | Mechanically → | Kinetic Store | Elastic Store | Gravitational Store |

At the start the gymnast is in the air above the springboard so the elastic store is empty, kinetic store has energy and the gravitational store has energy. At the end, the springboard is compressed and the gymnast has a moment where they are stationary. So the elastic store has energy, gravitational store has a little energy and the kinetic store is empty.

*Exam hint: Look at the question to work out what stores are involved to select the right formula for calculations.*

69

## P7.1.4: Energy Analysis with Forces 3

If you imagine a situation where you throw a ball up in the air:
Initially the ball is moving up and is quite close to the Earth so there is some GPE and some kinetic energy. When the ball reaches its peak it comes to a momentary stop so has no kinetic energy and lots of GPE as it is high off the ground.

The <u>energy analysis diagram</u> would look like this:

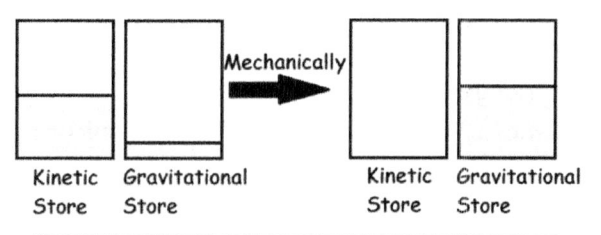

| Kinetic Store | Gravitational Store | → Mechanically | Kinetic Store | Gravitational Store |

*Exam hint: Remember acceleration due to gravity is $10m/s^2$.*

Remember that because some energy is transferred to the thermal store by friction, the ball will not reach the maximum height possible. Our energy analysis diagram should include a thermal store too.

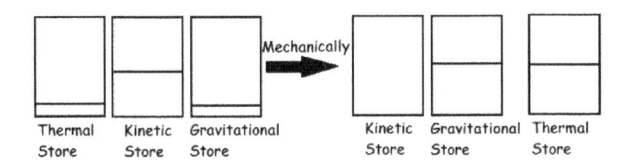

| Thermal Store | Kinetic Store | Gravitational Store | →Mechanically→ | Kinetic Store | Gravitational Store | Thermal Store |

## Check Your Understanding

1. List the 8 energy stores.

2. List the 4 energy transfers.

3. What formula would you use to calculate kinetic energy?

4. What formula would you use to calculate gravitational potential energy?

5. Draw an energy analysis diagram for a car in a drag race.

6. A drag racer comes to a stop over 50m. Calculate the force exerted by the brakes. The energy in the kinetic store before braking is $1.2 \times 10^6$ J.

# P7.2.1: Energy, Power and Paying for Electricity

Energy is transferred when charge moves from a battery or power station.

The energy store in a battery is a chemical store.

The energy store in a power plant is either a chemical store or a nuclear store, depending on the type of power plant.

Electrons in the wire produce light, a heating effect or make a motor turn to transfer energy.

Electrical devices have a power rating in watts (W) or kilowatts (kW).

Power: The rate of transfer of energy or the work done/time.

In our homes, the energy transferred by electrical appliances is measured with an electricity meter.

The meters use the kilowatt-hour as the unit of energy. A unit is the energy transferred by a 1kW appliance when it is on for 1 hour.

**Work Done (kWh) = Power (kW) x Time (h)**

**Power (W) = Work Done (J) ÷ Time (s)**

*Exam hint: If you are asked to calculate the cost of running an appliance then work out the units used first and then multiply this by the cost per unit.*

# P7.2.2: Energy Analysis - Electric Current

An electrical appliance transfers energy from chemical stores to other stores electrically.

E.g.

Hairdryers dry your hair by using the energy:
- Transferred electrically to produce heating by radiation
- Transferred mechanically to move the fan and air

If the device being used has a higher power rating, the amount of fuel it needs to run it is greater than that needed for a lower power device.

This means it will carry out jobs faster but uses more fuel to do it.

When current flows in a wire, the wire heats up. This means energy is transferred to a thermal store when you use an electrical appliance. This energy is wasted.

> *Exam hint: Remember that if you are asked to calculate energy changes when heating water, you will need the specific heat capacity formula from the data sheet.*

## P7.2.3: Energy Analysis – Heating

Energy in a thermal store is increased by heating, usually by:
- Burning a fuel
- Using electric current to transfer energy from a fuel

<u>If a temperature difference exists between two objects, energy transfer occurs. The hot object (source) transfers energy to the colder object (sink) until they are at equilibrium.</u> The rate of transfer is faster when the temperature difference is greater.

<u>Storage heaters contain concrete</u> which heats up when the heating is on and then releases the stored energy through the day when the heating is off. This can be a cost-effective way of heating if you have an energy plan that costs less overnight.

<u>Dissipation: The transfer of energy to stores that are not useful which cannot be used for working or heating.</u>

E.g. friction between moving parts leads to those parts heating up.

Ultimately, energy will end up in the thermal store of the surroundings.

<u>Dissipation can be reduced by:</u>
- <u>Lubricating items</u> – Reduces dissipation by friction by placing a layer of fluid between two solid surfaces which prevents direct contact.
- <u>Insulating items</u> – Reduces dissipation by heating by placing a poor conductor between a hot object and a cold one which reduces the rate of energy transfer.

# P7.2.4: Walls and Insulation

When it is cold, we use the heating in our homes to keep them warm. If the heating is turned off, the house cools down as energy is transferred to the surroundings via windows, walls etc.

The rate at which energy is transferred through the walls depends upon their thickness, the material they are made of and the temperature difference between inside and outside.

Most houses there are two layers of stone or brick with insulation between. This is a cavity wall.

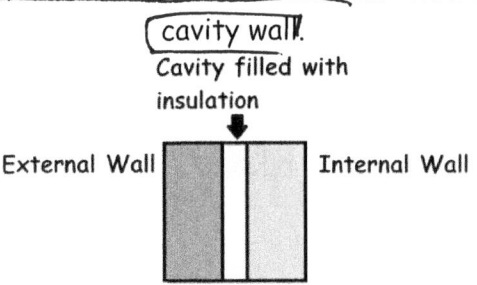

Cavity filled with insulation

External Wall    Internal Wall

Thermal conductivity of a material tells you the rate at which it transfers energy though a wall with:
- An area of 1m$^2$
- A thickness of 1m
- A temperature difference of 1$^O$C

The higher the thermal conductivity, the faster the material transfers energy and therefore leads to faster cooling.

To reduce the rate of cooling:
- Have thicker walls
- How lower thermal conductivity of the materials used to make them or insulate them

## P7.2.5: Efficiency

An efficient device is better at transferring energy between stores that do the job we want.

**Efficiency = (Useful Output Energy ÷ Input Energy) x 100**

*Exam hint: Think about the intended use of the object to identify which energy type is useful and which is wasted.*

E.g. A lamp has an input of 100J. The output to light is 60J and the output to heat is 40J. Calculate the efficiency of the light bulb.

Useful Energy = Light = 60J
Wasted Energy = Heat = 40J
Efficiency = (60 ÷ 100) x 100
=60%

**Sankey diagrams** are used to show the efficiency. The **width of the arrow** shows the amount of energy transferred.

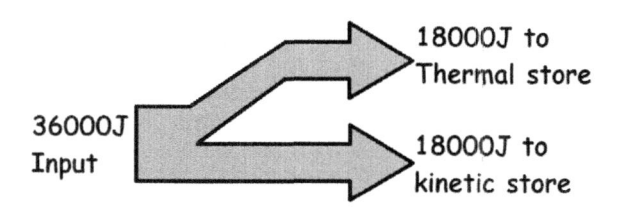

36000J Input → 18000J to Thermal store / 18000J to kinetic store

**To increase efficiency, you must reduce the wasted energy.**
This can be achieved by:
- **Insulating**
- Using materials that **reduce unwanted energy transfer**
- Use **improved** technology e.g. LED

More efficient devices operate at a lower power so use fuels more slowly.

# Check Your Understanding

1. What does the power rating tell us?

2. What is the formula for calculating the work done by an appliance?

3. Explain the energy transfers in a hairdryer

4. Define the term dissipation.

5. Explain how you can reduce the amount of energy dissipated in an object.

6. Explain how to reduce the energy transfers from your home to the surroundings.

7. How do you calculate efficiency?

8. How can you increase efficiency?

# P8 Global Challenges

## P8.1.1: Speed

There are a range of instruments we use to measure speed in our everyday lives. These include speed cameras, speed guns, electronic timers and satnav systems.

If you consider how the distance is measured, it may be using a tape measure, trundle wheel or by comparing the distance to different satellites.

To work out the time we may use an electronic timer, the time between two photos or pressure sensors to start a timer and a laser being broken to end it.

> **Speed (m/s) = Distance (m) ÷ Time (s)**

You need to know some typical speeds of objects in everyday situations. Here is a selection:
- A person walking = 1m/s (2.2mph)

- A person running = 5m/s (11mph)
  - A cyclist = 7m/s (15mph)
  - A car = 22m/s (50mph)
- Sound = 330m/s (738mph)

> *Exam hint: Make sure you know at least one fast and one slow object. You can then estimate others.*

You may also be asked to use the acceleration formula in everyday situations.

> **Acceleration (m/s$^2$) = Change in Speed (m/s) ÷ Time (s)**

When talking about data, we may see these terms used:

Precise: Data has a small range when repeated.

Accurate: Close to the true value.

## P8.1.2: Reaction Time and Thinking Distance

Reaction Time = Time taken from seeing something to the reaction (putting on the brake or pressing the stopwatch button).

Human reaction time is about 0.2 seconds.

Reaction times can be measured by dropping a ruler and catching it or by using a reaction time tester on the computer.

Thinking Distance = Distance travelled in the time it takes from seeing a potential problem to starting to apply the brakes.

> *Exam hint: Don't forget it is a DISTANCE so it is how far you travel in the time it takes to react.*

Thinking distance will be increased by:
- Drinking alcohol
- Using drugs
- Being tired
- Distractions
- Eating or drinking
- Using a sat nav or radio or mobile phone
- Increased speed

*Exam hint: Thinking distance is anything that impacts on the person and their ability to react.*

*Exam hint: Drugs and alcohol usually are classed as the same marking point so only use one of those.*

## P8.1.3: Braking Distance and Stopping Distance

Braking Distance = Distance travelled in the time it takes from putting the foot on the brake to coming to a stop.

*Exam hint: Don't forget it is a DISTANCE so it is how far you travel in the time it takes to stop.*

Factors that increase the braking distance:
- Increased speed
- Icy or wet roads
- Poor brake condition
- Poor tyre condition

*Exam hint: Braking distance is about a factor that impacts on the car*

Stopping Distance = Total distance travelled from the moment the driver sees the problem to coming to a stop.

Stopping Distance = Thinking Distance + Braking Distance

If we consider how speed affects the thinking and braking distance, they both increase with increased speed. However, thinking distance <u>increases in a linear fashion</u>.

E.g. 20mph = 6m
30mph = 9m
40mph = 12m

It increases by 3m for every 10mph.

| Speed | Thinking | Braking | Stopping |
|-------|----------|---------|----------|
| 20mph | 6 | 6 | 12 |
| 30mph | 9 | 14 | 23 |
| 40mph | 12 | 24 | 36 |
| 50mph | 15 | 38 | 53 |
| 60mph | 18 | 55 | 73 |
| 70mph | 21 | 75 | 96 |

## P8.1.4: Forces in Collisions

When <u>wearing a seatbelt</u> and the car comes to a sudden stop, you move forward and the seatbelt stretches and brings you to a <u>slower stop</u>. This <u>reduces the forces acting on your body</u>. Seatbelts need replacing after a crash as they have been stretched.

When not wearing a seatbelt and the car comes to a sudden stop, you continue to move forwards at the original speed until something stops you.

If the negative acceleration is very large, you can suffer compression injuries from the seatbelt or the internal organs can be damaged as they collide with the ribs.

The maximum speed on a motorway in the UK is 70mph.

The force you experience from a collision on the motorway will depend on the amount of time the collision takes. The longer it takes to bring you to a stop, the lower the force acting on your body will be.

**Force (N) = Mass (kg) x Acceleration (m/s$^2$)**

Cars have certain features, in addition to the seatbelt, that are there to reduce the forces acting on your in a crash. They include:
- Crumple zones
- Air bags

# Check Your Understanding

1. How would you measure the distance in a 100m race?

2. How would you measure the time in a speed camera?

3. What is the typical speed of a person walking?

4. What is the typical speed of a person running?

5. List three factors that increase thinking distance.

6. List three factors that increase braking distance.

7. Explain why you should wear a seatbelt in cars.

# P8.2.1: Energy Sources

An energy source is something we can use for heating, transportation or generating electricity.

Energy sources are either renewable or non-renewable.

Renewable: Will not run out.

Non-Renewable: Will run out. Being used faster than it is being made.

Renewable energy sources:
- Biofuels
- Solar
- Tides
- Wind
- Waves
- Geothermal
- Hydroelectric

Non-renewable energy sources:
- Fossil Fuels – Coal, oil and natural gas
  - Nuclear fuels

Nuclear fuels were formed in stars.

Fossil fuels were formed from the effects of pressure and temperature on the remains of living things over millions of years.

There are three main uses of energy sources:
1. Heating E.g. fossil fuels; biofuels, Sun and geothermal
2. Transportation E.g. Fossil fuels and biofuels
3. Generating Electricity

We can also heat our houses by:
- Building houses that maximise heat from the sun.
- Use solar panels
- Use hot water from underground (in some areas)

We can generate electricity by:
- Using photovoltaic cells (solar cells)
- Use turbines and generators driven by wind, waves, geothermal, hydroelectric or biofuels.

# P8.2.2: Using Resources

The use of energy sources over time has changed because there has been an increase in population, our use of devices has changed, and we use more electricity. This results in increased electricity generation and increased use of devices that use fuels.

The supply of fossil fuels is finite – They will run out.

There are reserves of fossil fuels in many parts of the world that are hard to reach. The harder fossil fuels are to find and extract, the more expensive they become.

<u>Burning fossil fuels produces the gas carbon dioxide. This leads to climate change and the greenhouse effect.</u>

Climate change leads to:
- Ice caps melting
- Sea levels rise
- Flooding
- Extreme weather events
- Threats to food supplies

When a government decides what energy source to use, they need to consider:
- Cost
- Environmental impact
- How long the sources will last

# P8.2.3: The National Grid

The National Grid is the system of cables, power stations, transformers and sub-stations that transport electricity across the country.

Transformers change the voltage (p.d.) to reduce the heating effect.

Step-Up transformers: Increase the p.d. or voltage.

Step-Down transformers: Decrease the p.d. or voltage.

If the wires heat up, energy is lost to the surroundings. The amount of heating depends on:
- Current
- Resistance

The more energy lost in transmission, means more fossil fuels must be burnt in the power station. Therefore, we should try to reduce energy losses in transmission.

When talking about transformers, you need to be able to use the formula from the Physics Formula Sheet:
$$V_p \times I_p = V_s \times I_s$$

E.g. Calculate the current in the secondary coil of your phone charger if it has a p.d. of 230V across the primary coil, 12 V across the secondary coil and a current of 0.1A in the primary coil.

$$I_s = (V_p \times I_p) \div V_s$$
$$= (230 \times 0.1) \div 12$$
$$= 1.9A$$

When a current is induced in the wires, they heat up. When the wires heat up, the iron core of the transformer also heats up. This transfers energy to the thermal store of the surroundings.

The amount of heating depends on the resistance of the wires and the size of the current.

To minimise energy loss due to this heating effect, a high potential difference is used. This means the current is lower and therefore less energy is lost via heating.

## P8.2.4: Mains Electricity

Mains electricity has a voltage of 230V. Generators in power stations create an alternating voltage with a frequency of 50Hz. This reaches our houses through the National Grid.

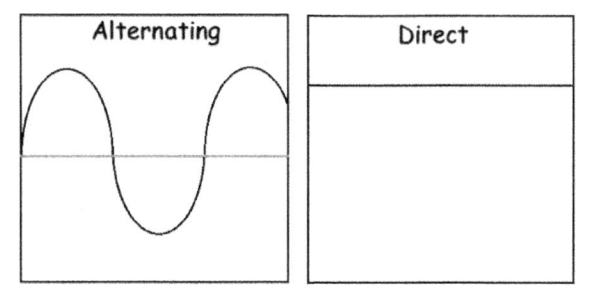

| Alternating | Direct |
|---|---|

Batteries create a direct voltage.

In the UK, our plugs have three wires inside. The live (brown) and neutral (blue) wire make a complete circuit with the appliance. The earth (yellow and green) wire is connected to earth.

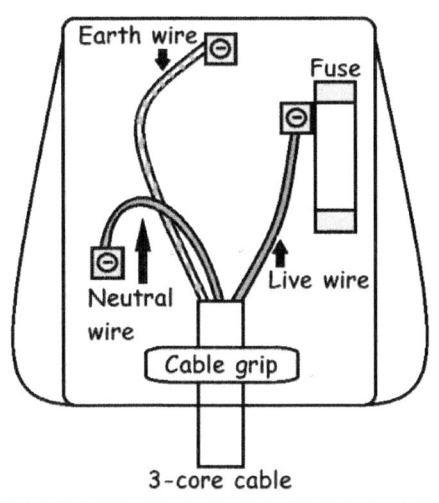

| Voltmeter between | Potential Difference |
| --- | --- |
| Live and Neutral | 230V |
| Live and Earth | 230V |
| Neutral and Earth | 0V |

We have a few key safety features inside our plugs to reduce the risk of electrocution.

If the live wire comes loose and touches the metal case on an appliance, it becomes live and you could be electrocuted. The earth wire connects to the case and the earth pole so the current flows into the earth wire and not you as it has less resistance than you do. The fuse will also melt to break the circuit and stop the current flowing.

Double insulated appliances: Case is plastic so no current can flow through the case to you. These do not need an earth.

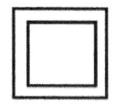

## Check Your Understanding

1. Explain the difference between renewable and non-renewable.

2. Give two examples of renewable energy sources.

3. Give two examples of non-renewable energy sources.

4. Explain why our use of energy sources has changed over the past 150 years.

5. Explain the problems of burning fossil fuels.

6. Explain how electricity is transmitted from the power station to our home.

7. Describe how a UK plug is wired.

## P8.3.1: The Big Bang

Over the history of human existence, our ideas about the Universe have changed. Here is a brief overview of some key parts:

- 400BC Aristotle: Earth was the centre of the Universe.
- 100AD Ptolemy: Earth centred model and the Universe was surrounded by a background of fixed, unchanging stars.
- 1543AD Copernicus: Sun-centred model
- 1609AD Galileo: Stars changed and not all objects orbit Earth
- 1687AD Newton: Theory of Gravity confirms sun-centric model.

Ideas about the Universe have changed as observations have been made and creative thinking occurred to explain the observations.

In 1929, Edwin Hubble measured speed of galaxies from the absorption spectrum of the light they emit.

When a light source moves away from you, the wavelength of the light it emits increases and the frequency decreases. This is red-shift.
- If the source is moving faster, the red-shift is bigger.
- If the source is moving towards you, the light is blue-shifted.

Hubble used red-shift to work out that galaxies were moving away from us. He also worked out that the more distant a galaxy is, the faster it is moving away.

To explain the origins of our Universe, the most widely accepted model is the Big Bang model. It states that the Universe started as something very dense and tiny (smaller than an atom) which underwent sudden expansion 13.7 billion years ago.

From that point to the present day, the space between the galaxies is expanding.

Contrary to what some people think, we are not at the centre of the Universe.

There are two <u>key pieces of evidence for the Big Bang theory:</u>

1) <u>Cosmic Microwave Background Radiation (CMBR)</u>

In the 1960s, astronomers found that microwave radiation came from all directions. The scientists worked out it was radiation left over from the Big Bang. The very high energy and high frequency radiation has been stretched over time so it is now in the microwave region of the EM spectrum.

## 2) Red-shift

The fact that the galaxies are moving away from each other with those furthest away moving quickest, supports the idea that in the distant past everything started in a central point of the Universe.

## P8.3.2: Our Solar System

The Solar System consists of:
- Sun (Star)
- Planets (Spherical objects in orbit around the Sun)
- Moons (Orbit around planets)
- Minor planets (Anything not a planet or comet in orbit around the Sun – asteroids and dwarf planets)
- Comets (Made of ice and dust that orbit the sun)

The inner planets are <u>Mercury, Venus, Earth and Mars.</u> <u>They are all rocky</u> and <u>have an atmosphere</u>. They do have key differences:
- <u>Mercury and Mars</u> have <u>very thin atmospheres</u> whereas Venus has an atmosphere that is mainly carbon dioxide and it rains sulphuric acid.
- <u>Earth has 1 moon; Mars has 2 moons; Mercury and Venus have no moons.</u>

The outer planets are Jupiter, Saturn, Uranus and Neptune.

Jupiter and Saturn are gas giants whereas Uranus and Neptune are ice giants. They all have rings and lots of moons.

The asteroid belt is between Mars and Jupiter. Asteroids are pieces of rock left over from the formation of the Solar System. The asteroid belt also contains a dwarf planet called Ceres.

The Sun formed from a huge cloud of dust and gas that was pulled together by gravity. As this happened, the core got very hot. Eventually the particles moved fast enough for nuclear fusion to occur. There is a balance between gravity pulling the particles inwards and the expansion of the hot gases outwards.

Formation of stars:
- A huge cloud of gas (mainly hydrogen) called a nebula begins to be pulled together by gravity.
- A large ball of gas forms at the centre of the cloud. As it gets denser, more gas is pulled in. The ball gets hotter and hotter, forming a proto-star.
- The proto-star continues to grow larger until nuclear fusion occurs and this is the main sequence star. This is the stable part of the lifecycle.

What happens when a star runs out of fuel to fuse depends upon the mass of the star.

Small Stars (our Sun):
- Cool and expand to become a red giant.
- Outer layers of the star break away to form a planetary nebula.
- The white-hot core of the star is all that remains = White dwarf. This cools over time.

Large Stars:
- Expand and cool but grow much larger to become red supergiants.
- The star explodes as a supernova.
- During the supernova, the core of the star is crushed down by immense gravitational forces to form a very dense star made of neutrons = Neutron star.
- The neutron star spins very fast and sends pulses of radio waves to Earth.

If the star is even bigger, the core is crushed down into a tiny space to form a black hole.

## P8.3.3: Satellites and Orbits

Satellites can be either natural or artificial.

Natural satellites are made of the same material as the rest of the objects in the Solar System e.g. moons

Artificial satellites are ones sent by humans to orbit objects like the Sun or planets.

We use two types of orbit for the satellites around Earth:
1) Geostationary orbit
2) Low Polar Orbit

Natural satellites have different orbits from the artificial satellites.

Geostationary Orbit:
Time for one orbit – 24 hours
Height above Earth's surface - ~36,000km
Features – Remains in fixed position above the Earth's equator.
Uses – Communications and satellite TV

Low Polar Orbit:
Time for one orbit – ~2 hours
Height above Earth's surface – up to 2000km
Features – Orbits over the poles
Uses – Military (spy); Observation on Earth; Weather

Stable orbits occur when the object is moving at the right speed for the distance from the object it orbits. E.g. planets. <u>As you move further from the Sun, the planets move slower</u>. This is because the <u>pull of gravity from the Sun is lower</u> as it is further so there is only a small force changing its velocity.

If a planet was to speed up, the gravitational force would be too small to keep it in orbit and so it would fly off.

If a planet was the slow down, it would accelerate towards the Sun.

## P8.3.4: Radiation and Temperature

All objects emit EM radiation. Warm objects will emit infrared radiation which we can detect with a thermal imaging camera.

The type of radiation emitted depends on the temperature of the object.

Hotter objects emit more radiation of a higher frequency and shorter wavelength, and less radiation of a lower frequency and longer wavelength.

By analysing the light from stars, a graph of intensity of radiation against frequency can be plotted. Hot stars have:
- Higher frequency
- Higher intensity

If an object emits the same amount of radiation as it absorbs, the temperature remains constant.

If more radiation is emitted than absorbed, it will cool down.

If more radiation is absorbed than emitted, the temperature will increase.

Earth absorbs radiation from the Sun and emits radiation into space. The Earth's atmosphere reflects some radiation back to Earth. The concentration of greenhouse gases in the atmosphere will determine the type and intensity of radiation reflected back. If greenhouse gases increase in concentration, the Earth will increase in temperature.

# P8.3.5: Inside Our Planet

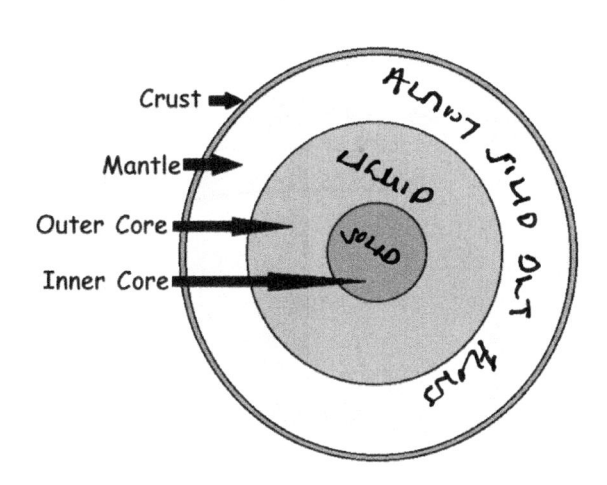

Crust → (Solid)
Mantle → (Almost solid but flows)
Outer Core → (Liquid)
Inner Core → (Solid)

Inner Core: Solid
Outer Core: Liquid
Mantle: Almost entirely solid but flows
Crust: Solid

We can't drill into the core to study it as it is too deep and too hot.

Earthquakes produce seismic waves which are detected on seismometers. Seismograms record the arrival and intensity of two types of seismic wave:
- P-waves (Primary)
- S-waves (Secondary)

Near the epicentre of an earthquake, both S-waves and P-waves are detected.

Some regions of the Earth are called shadow zones where P-waves or S-waves or neither can be detected.

P-waves are longitudinal waves and can travel through solids and liquids.

S-waves are transverse waves and cannot travel through liquids. (S=Solid)

Bruno Gutenberg stated that this means the core must be liquid in 1914.

In 1936, Inge Lehmann analysed P-waves and worked out that the very centre is solid. (Inner core)

By analysing seismic waves, we have now worked out the sizes of the inner and outer core.

# Check Your Understanding

1) Explain what red-shift is.

2) Explain the evidence for the Big Bang model.

3) Describe the objects within our Solar System.

4) Where is the asteroid belt?

5) Describe the life cycle of small stars.

6) Describe the differences between the two orbits satellites can be held in.

7) Describe the structure of the Earth.

8) Explain how the structure of the Earth has been worked out.

# About Wright Science

Wright Science is a YouTube channel created by Vicki Wright, a secondary science teacher in England.

I started Wright Science as a resource for my own classes to have extra help outside of school time.  It started with a single recap video for each exam back in 2013 and then just grew.  These days there are videos for every lesson on both the separate science courses and combined science courses which are used by a number of students across the country and world!

I hope that you find this book useful and welcome your comments.

Good luck in your exams!

Printed in Great Britain
by Amazon